747.77
Jen
P6

Lynette Jennings

have fun with your room

28 COOL PROJECTS FOR TEENS

ALADDIN PAPERBACKS

NEW YORK   LONDON   TORONTO   SYDNEY   SINGAPORE

LYNETTE JENNINGS

First Aladdin Paperbacks edition
October 2001

ALADDIN PAPERBACKS
An imprint of Simon & Schuster
Children's Publishing Division
1230 Avenue of the Americas
New York, NY 10020

Designed by Anne Scatto / PIXEL PRESS

The text of this book was set in Helvetica

Printed and bound in
the United States of America

10 9 8 7 6 5 4 3 2 1

CIP Data for this book is available from
the Library of Congress.

ISBN 0-689-82585-4

Flower Power

1

introduction..........................

WOULDN'T YOU JUST LOVE TO DO something really neat to your room—something cool, something totally YOU?

Well, you can!

(*LET'S TRY THAT AGAIN.*) **YOU** can.

Yes, You **CAN!!!**

After all, it **IS** *your* room.

Need a lot of $$$$$?
Nope!

Need a **BIGGER** room?

No more space than you already have.

Need a whole bunch of tools? Not really. Most of what we used you probably have around the house. Ask your parents.

You can make all of our projects yourself, with basic tools and household items. (Except for a few times when you might need help cutting wood, which you can easily get at home or even at a home improvement store.)

Need a lot of help from Mom and Dad? Not unless you'd like to let them in on your project! Except when it comes to changing the wall color or painting a piece of your furniture, you need their permission, of course.

NOW, HOW CAN YOU DECORATE your room all by yourself!? After all, you've probably seen your parents work long and hard on their decorating and renovation projects. And decorating a room sounds like it takes a lot of work, money, and imagination. Right? Sometimes that's true. But not this time! We decorated the four bedrooms in this book *on a baby-sitter's budget,* just to show *you* how you can turn *your* bedroom into a very special place that's *your* style.

Does it matter what your furniture looks like right now? No. In fact, we used pretty typical kids' room furniture that didn't match, just so you wouldn't feel you had to have expensive designer stuff to get a great-looking room.

SO LET'S GET STARTED....

FIRST STEP *HOW DO YOU WANT YOUR ROOM TO LOOK?*

If you're thinking

> "I dunno, I don't have any idea! Just fun, funky, cool. But I have lots of old teddy bears I'm not willing to give up."

or

> "It's time to ditch my little-girl thing. I want pure MTV!"

or

> "I'm the outdoorsy type. Don't really care much for frilly stuff. Just want something less little-girl-ish."

What you are really doing is beginning to decide your style.

In decorating terms, if you just throw a bunch of things into the room without coordinating the colors or the theme (kind of like a party), it doesn't look "together" or "coordinated" or "styled." Sort of like wearing biking shorts with a pajama top. Whoops! Hard to explain why that doesn't work—it just looks weird.

So to help you out, we put these four rooms together based on four different personalities. Which one looks like you?

At this point, you'll either know:

which one is *absolutely* YOU,

or

that none of them is,

or

that there are a few things in each one you really like.

Hey, that's okay. And here's why. No two bedrooms are alike. And no two teenagers are alike with exactly the same stuff. So you need to adapt these ideas to **YOUR LOOK,** in your favorite colors.

How do you start? Well, you can get out your stuff and dive right in, or you can think a bit about what your style might be. Dream a little. Here's a little help:

Answer this fun questionnaire to find YOUR style

1.

WHEN IT'S YOUR TURN TO CHOOSE A VIDEO, YOU BRING HOME

a) Discovery's underwater tour.

b) a rock video or fashion TV reruns.

c) romantic chick-flicks.

d) anything, as long as it has a happy ending.

2.

AFTER SCHOOL YOU STOP FOR ICE CREAM. WHICH FLAVOR DO YOU CHOOSE?

a) fat-free rainbow sherbet

b) peanut butter–brownie–marshmallow–caramel crunchy chunk

c) strawberry bubble gum with Smarties

d) chocolate

3.

Your best friend is having a Halloween party. Which of the following characters would you go as?

a) a tree, a butterfly, or a cat

b) a bass player in an all-girl rock band, a trendy fashion queen, or a techno dancer

c) a birthday package, a chocolate Hershey's Kiss, or a cheerleader

d) a princess, a ballerina, or a mermaid

4.

YOUR FAVORITE SHADE OF NAIL POLISH IS

a) clear.

b) purple with silver sparkles.

c) a different shade of red, orange, and yellow on each finger.

d) pastel pinks, blues, and greens.

5. YOUR SCHOOL LOCKER

a) has very little in it, just what you need for class.

b) has everything in it, including one lost gym sock, a leftover lunch in one of Mom's plastic containers, a broken CD case, and a boyfriend's fleece jacket.

c) has lots of hangers and organizing gadgets, including a mirror that your friends gave you for your last birthday 'cause you're a neatnik.

d) has a sweater, candy, books, and pictures of your friends taped to the inside door.

6.

By Saturday morning your room can best be described as

a) an out-of-control laboratory of school experiments and a gerbil cage needing to be cleaned.

b) a disaster.

c) totally neat and organized, even though it's Saturday.

d) a rumpled bed full of cozy socks, Judy Blume books, jammies, and half a bag of chocolate chip cookies.

7.

YOUR FAVORITE DREAM HOLIDAY WOULD BE

a) hiking in the Himalayas.

b) a week on tour in London with your favorite rock group.

c) shopping on Manhattan's Fifth Avenue.

d) cruising the Caribbean on a "Love Boat."

NOW LET'S LOOK AT THE ANSWERS and see how your room might look. You probably won't have a perfect score. But you'll have a better idea of how your personality can influence your room.

ANSWERS:

If your answers are mostly **(a)**, you'll probably feel right at home in our **NATURE GIRL** room. Turn to page 44 to see this room and all the terrific projects you can make to create it.

If your answers are mostly **(b)**, our **FUNKY CHICK** room is your digs. Turn to page 34 for the scoop on this room.

If your answers are mostly **(c)**, our **FLOWER POWER** room will look good on you. Turn to page 1 to check it out.

If your answers are mostly **(d)**, our **TEDDY BEARS** room will warm your heart. Turn to page 16 and snuggle up in its coziness.

DECORATING ANY ROOM IN THE house, whether you are a kid like yourself, a grown-up, or even a professional, starts with these steps.

Find your style. Pretend you're going to **wear** your room!! Sounds silly, but it's remarkable how often people's houses are decorated in their wardrobe styles—and it suits them.

Decide on your favorite colors. Don't think twice, just blurt them out. If you think too long, you'll get all confused. **Then go for it!!!**

Clean up your room and get rid of yucky stuff. Don't throw away anything you **just love**. And it's okay to put some things away for a while. You never know when you'll want them. But some-times a lifetime of collecting stuff gets to be a little much (unless you can recycle it with paint).

Can't figure out what your room could look like? Try closing your eyes and imagining one corner at a time. Much easier.

Make a list of what you want to do and when you're going to do it. Everybody has great ideas. And then they evaporate in the shower, over dinner, while you're sleeping. Pouf! All that genius, gone. Write your ideas down. Even draw a picture. You don't have to show it to anyone. Then decide between homework, babysitting, or chores just what and when you're going to do whatever.

Decide how much your project is going to cost. You might need a little help with this one. But, hey, you can do a lot of this yourself. Make a list of the materials and phone around.

Do one project at a time. The absolute worst thing you can do is to try starting lots of projects at once. CHAOS! E E E C H h h h h h h h h ! And take your time, have fun. Watch out for "project frenzy." Symptoms: big grin or wrinkled brow, over-excitement, hands moving too quickly, glue spilling, paint splattering, hands shaking in excitement, music too loud, ignoring parent's call, ignoring pesky siblings. Slow down, take care.

And have lots of fun doing it!

MOST IMPORTANT:
Don't worry about the goofs!!

Decorating is not a perfect science. It's art and it's personal. Don't let other people tell you something you do looks dumb or uncool. If *you* like it, *do it!* It's your room, not theirs! Got it?

NOW, COME ON. LET'S GET AT THAT ROOM OF YOURS. . . .

Power

You're a rainbow of delights. Our "Flower Power" room will look good on you. The original shop-till-you-drop girl. Lunching with your friends. Rainbows, hearts, and flowers in jelly pens are your favorite scribble, of course, along with writing your boyfriend's name ten different ways.

flowered window shade

WHAT YOU'LL NEED

White vinyl window shade

Tracing paper

Pencil

Acrylic paints or large paint markers: lime green, hot pink, yellow, turquoise

1" foam brushes

Splat  Splat

Let's Get Started

Woodstik

BROAD TIP

FOR DECORATING ANYTHING ON WOOD

go to page 56 for a traceable flower template

1 Spread out the shade and weight it down with books on the edges so it doesn't roll up (flap, flap, flap . . . !).

2 Trace our flower design from page 56 with tracing paper and a pencil to make a paper pattern. You can shrink and enlarge the pattern on a photocopier to the size you want for your window shade, but it's even more fun to draw your own flowers!

3 Draw in a row of flowers along the bottom of the shade. Don't forget the centers!

4 Paint all of the flower petals bright colors. Let dry. Now paint the centers with other bright colors. Let dry. Add swirly lines to the flower centers with the yellow marker.

5 With the lime green marker, make two squiggly lines horizontally above your flowers. Then take the yellow marker and make more squiggly lines going vertically along the window shade.

6 Let your project dry overnight and get a parent to help you hang it up.

flowered Headboard

WHAT YOU'LL NEED

Masonite or Fome-Cor board, cut to size of bed

Ruler or tape measure

Sandpaper

White paint

1" foam brush

Large paint markers in cool colors: lime green, purple, yellow, melon, turquoise

Tracing paper

Pencil

Small nails and picture-frame hanging hooks

Hammer

Let's Get Started

1 Lay out your board and mark off the dimensions for your headboard. It should be as wide as your bed. Get someone to cut it for you—at home or at a home improvement center. Smooth the edges of your board with sandpaper. Then use an old T-shirt or soft cloth to wipe it clean.

2 Paint your board white. Don't forget to paint around those edges, too. Let it dry as recommended on the paint can before applying a second coat. Let it dry completely, preferably overnight. Here's a tip: If you use Fome-Cor board, paint both sides—it keeps it from warping.

3 Take the large yellow marker to squiggle a bright border around your headboard. Our border is about 3 inches wide. Look at the photo for a guide. Let it dry before you start adding your flowers.

4 Trace the flower design on page 56 and make a paper pattern. Using a photocopier you can shrink and enlarge the pattern for different sizes of flowers.

5 Trace the flowers onto your board or draw them free-form. Don't be nervous. Do them in pencil first if you like. The sillier the flowers look, the better!

6 Paint the flower petals. Let them dry. Then add the centers with another bright paint color. Let dry.

7 Jazz up the flower centers by adding swirly lines with the yellow marker. Let your project dry overnight.

8 Attach your headboard to the wall with nails and picture-frame hooks.

Buttons AND Bows Pillow

WHAT YOU'LL NEED

Multicolored buttons

White pillowcase

Embroidery thread in bright colors

Embroidery needle

Scissors

Grosgrain ribbon, ⅝" wide, in 6 colors—
we used green, turquoise, pink,
orange, purple, and yellow

Let's Get Started

1 Sew the buttons onto the pillowcase. Use two strands of thread to attach the buttons firmly. Ask your mom to get you started if you've never sewn on buttons. It looks great if you use a different color embroidery thread with each button. Now you're ready to add the ribbons!

2 Cut the ribbon into 12-inch lengths. Make bows using different-colored ribbons. Sew the bows onto the pillowcases. Here's a tip: Sew through the center knot of each bow so it won't come untied.

ribbon lampshade

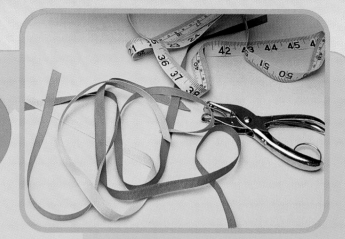

WHAT YOU'LL NEED

Lampshade

Pencil

Tape measure

Hole punch

Grosgrain ribbon, ⅝" wide, in six colors—we used purple, pink, lime green, yellow, turquoise, and melon

Let's Get Started

1 Using a pencil, make marks around the bottom of the lampshade about 1½ inches apart. This is where you will punch the holes. You need to make an even number of holes.

2 Punch holes where you've made pencil marks.

3 Cut the ribbon into 12-inch pieces. You will need one length of ribbon for every two holes. Start at the front of the lampshade and push a length of ribbon through the first hole and then loop it back through the next hole. Use the photo on the left as a guide. Now pull the ribbon so it's even and tie a pretty bow. Continue until you've threaded ribbon through all the holes.

RIBBON GOES IN FROM FRONT AND THROUGH INSIDE OF SHADE AND BACK OUT THE FRONT.

flower switch plate

WHAT YOU'LL NEED

A White switch plate

Silk flowers

Scissors

Hot glue gun and glue

OR

B White switch plate

Puff paint, or you can use paint pens—we used purple and teal

Let's Get Started

SILK FLOWER SWITCH PLATE
Clip your silk flowers as close to the base as possible with scissors. With the hot glue gun, put a small dab of glue on the back of each flower and place it on the switch plate.

PAINTED SWITCH PLATE
For a different look, paint on brightly colored flowers with markers or paint.

WHAT YOU'LL NEED

2-liter plastic soda bottle

Scissors

Plaster of Paris

Water

Mixing bowl

Measuring cup

1¼" PVC pipe, cut 10" long

Decorative wooden finial

Hot glue gun and glue or E6000 adhesive

Acrylic paint: lime green, purple, pink, yellow, and turquoise

Paint markers: yellow and white

Paintbrushes

With the scissors, cut the soda bottle in half horizontally. Save both pieces. Cut a hole in the top of the bottle large enough for the PVC pipe to fit through it tightly.

1

Let's Get Started

2

Mix the plaster of Paris in a mixing bowl, following the instructions on the package. Make sure to get all the lumps out. Pour 3 cups of the plaster mixture into the bottom of the soda bottle. Tap the soda bottle on the table to level out the plaster, or smooth it out with the wooden spoon.

Push the PVC pipe into the center of the plaster. Put the top of the soda bottle over the PVC pipe to hold it in place until it dries. Let it dry overnight.

3

4 Remove the top of the soda bottle from the pipe. Cut away the bottom of the soda bottle from the dry plaster base. Glue the wooden finial to the top of the PVC pipe with E6000 adhesive or a hot glue gun.

Paint away!!

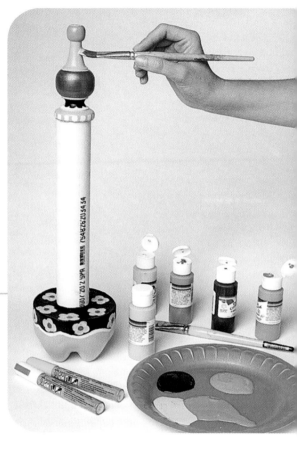

5 Paint the base and the top of your scrunchy post with brightly colored paint and markers.

stack some scrunchies!

chair pocket

WHAT YOU'LL NEED

Tape measure

1½ yards of felt

Pinking shears (these are scissors with jagged edges)

Scissors

Sewing machine

6 felt squares in bright colors for flowers (2 of each color)

2 yellow felt squares for flower centers

Fabric glue

1 Measure the depth of the chair seat (A) and the height of the chair seat from the floor (B), and the width of the chair seat (C). See diagram at right.

2 Using your measurements from above, add B + C + B to determine the length of the felt. A is the width of the felt. See diagram below.

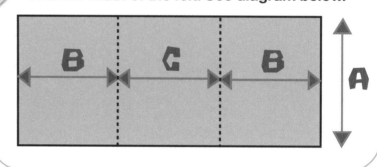

circles

3 To give it a really neat-looking edge, trim all sides with pinking shears. Place the felt across the chair and trim it to fit.

flowers

4 Cut two large felt squares (B" x A") to use as pockets on each side. Use diagram #2 as a guide.

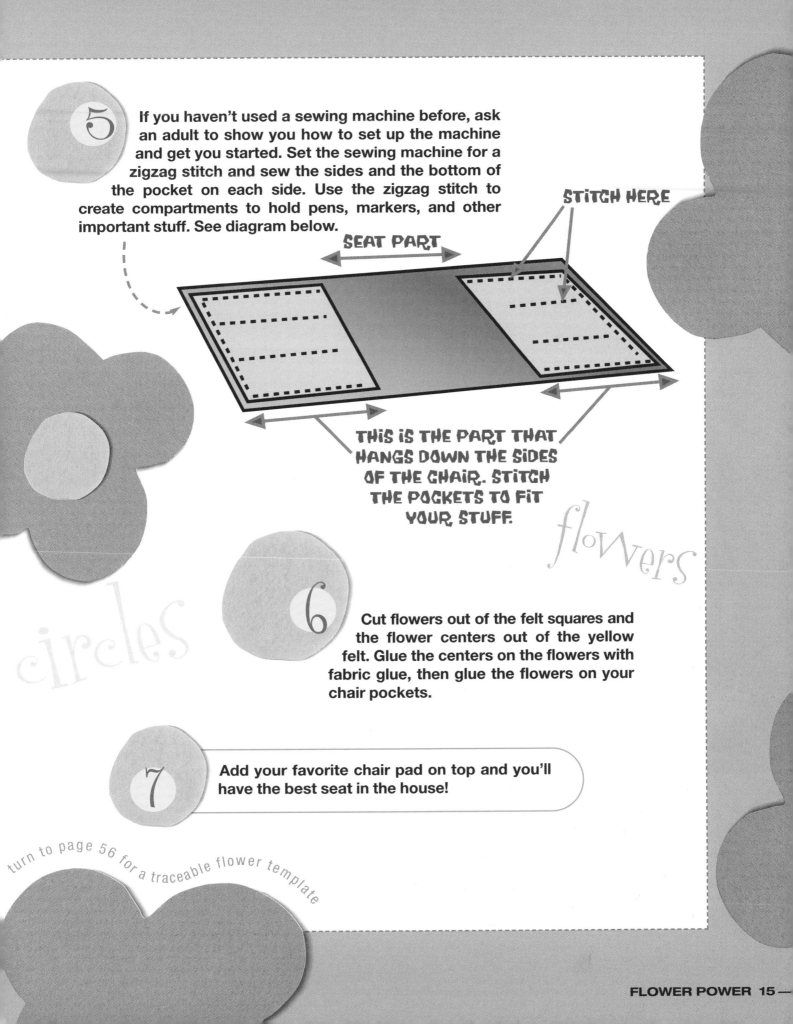

5 If you haven't used a sewing machine before, ask an adult to show you how to set up the machine and get you started. Set the sewing machine for a zigzag stitch and sew the sides and the bottom of the pocket on each side. Use the zigzag stitch to create compartments to hold pens, markers, and other important stuff. See diagram below.

STITCH HERE

SEAT PART

THIS IS THE PART THAT HANGS DOWN THE SIDES OF THE CHAIR. STITCH THE POCKETS TO FIT YOUR STUFF.

flowers

circles

6 Cut flowers out of the felt squares and the flower centers out of the yellow felt. Glue the centers on the flowers with fabric glue, then glue the flowers on your chair pockets.

7 Add your favorite chair pad on top and you'll have the best seat in the house!

turn to page 56 for a traceable flower template

Teddy Bears

You're well on your way to being a hopeless romantic. Snuggle, baby, in our milk chocolate garden of Teddy Bears. "Cozy" is your middle name. You curl up with your book and your cat on a rainy day. You know you have to grow up sometime, but you just can't bring yourself to stash Mr. Bear in the attic.

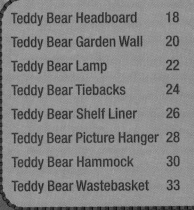

teddy Bear Headboard

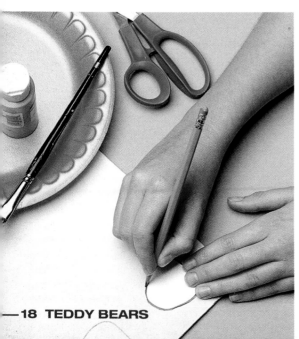

WHAT YOU'LL NEED

Masonite or Fome-Cor board

Ruler or tape measure

Sandpaper

Acrylic paint: cream, chocolate brown

1" foam brush

Tracing paper

Pencil

Biodegradable foam plates

Small paintbrushes

Nails and picture-frame hanging hooks

Hammer

2 small nails

1 wooden peg

4 yards of rope trim

Let's Get Started

1. **Prepare your headboard following the step #1 directions for the headboard on page 5. Or, if you want, you can paint this right on your wall!!!! Just use a tape measure and yardstick to create the rectangle and paint it cream.**

   Paint your headboard with cream paint. Don't forget to paint around those edges, too. Let it dry completely, preferably overnight. Here's a tip: If you use Fome-Cor board, you'll want to paint both sides—it keeps it from warping.

2. **With tracing paper, create a paper pattern for the teddy bear paw, using the one on page 55 as a guide.**

go to page 55 for a traceable paw print

3 Trace the center of the paw around your headboard and paint the paw with light chocolate brown paint. Get those fingers ready, because now you're going to finger paint! Pour the brown paint onto the foam plate. Then dip your index finger into it, and put three prints above the paw. Let it dry. While you've got your brown paint out, go ahead and paint your wooden peg. It will probably take two coats.

4 Write "I ♥ T-Bears" in the center of your border with a pencil. Grab your pink paint marker and make X's over the letters and inside the heart to make it look like cross-stitch. Draw a border around the heart in pink.

5 If you haven't painted your headboard right on the wall, you'll need to attach it to the wall with small nails and picture-frame hanging hooks. Now draw a pretty frame on the wall around your headboard with a pink marker.

←NAILS

6 Hammer a small nail in each top corner of your painted frame (see diagram).

7 Center the wooden peg about 6 inches above your headboard and screw it into the wall. Then take the rope and drape it over the wooden peg and nails at the top of the frame as shown in the diagram at right and the picture on page 18.

WHAT YOU'LL NEED

Tracing paper

Pencil

2 cellulose kitchen sponges

Black marker

Scissors

1 large rectangular cellulose sponge

Acrylic paint: gray, green, pink

Paint trays or plastic meat trays
  from the grocery

Drop cloth

Paper towels

teddy bear garden wall

Let's Get Started

turn to page 55 for a traceable vine

① Using tracing paper, make a pattern for your leaves and flowers with the templates on page 55. Next, place your leaf and flower patterns on top of the sponges, trace them with a marker, and cut them out.

② With scissors, trim the edges of the large rectangular sponge to create an uneven brick shape.

③ Soak the sponges in water and squeeze until they are slightly damp.

④ Start with your bricks. Decide where you want to create a brick wall in your room. Pour gray paint into a plastic tray. Make sure you put a drop cloth, plastic, or newspapers under your work area.

⑤ Dip your sponge into the paint and blot onto a paper towel.

⑥ Start with the bottom row and press the sponge on the wall. You will be able to get two or three presses before loading more paint onto your sponge. Be sure to blot it on a paper towel each time before going to the wall. Stagger the bricks on each row like we've done on our wall. Use the corners as your guide.

⑦ Repeat these steps until you've created a beautiful garden wall in your room. Let it dry for about 2 hours.

⑧ Repeat the same steps to "stamp" the flowers and vines on the wall with your sponge patterns.

Be creative and let them trail over the wall and around windows, shelves, and furniture.

flip to page 55 for a traceable flower

TEDDY BEAR LAMP

WHAT YOU'LL NEED

Lampshade—cream or white

Tracing paper

Pencil or black marker

2 kitchen sponges

Scissors

Water

Acrylic paint: brown, pink

Biodegradable foam plates

Paper towels

Let's Get Started

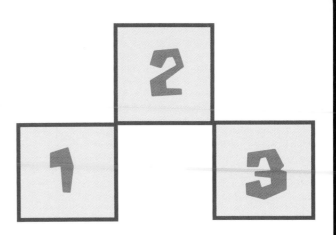

squares

 1 Using tracing paper, make a paper pattern using the design on this page to create the heart and squares. Trace each pattern on top of a sponge with a pencil or black marker and cut them out.

2 Soak the sponges in water and squeeze until they are slightly damp.

3 Pour paint onto the foam plate. Use a paper towel as a blotter. Start with the squares. Dip the squares sponge into brown paint and blot on the paper towel. Using the photo as a guide, make two rows of checks on the top and bottom of the lampshade.

4 Repeat the steps for painting the hearts with pink paint. Make a row of hearts around the middle of the lampshade. Let dry overnight.

heart

WHAT YOU'LL NEED

1 sheet of poster board

Tape measure

Pencil

½ yard of fabric—we used pink

Scissors

HeatnBond iron-on glue tape, ⅜" wide

Iron

Hot glue gun and glue

Small teddy bears of different shapes and sizes

4 plastic curtain rings

Needle and thread

2 cup hooks

teddy bear tiebacks

Let's Get Started

1 Measure out and cut two pieces of poster board 10 inches wide and 18 inches long. Fold each piece into thirds lengthwise and flatten. This makes your tieback nice and stiff.

Next cut two pieces of fabric 14 inches wide and 22 inches long. Lay out your fabric and place the folded poster board in the middle. Put a piece of HeatnBond across one side of the poster board and press down with an iron (follow package instructions). Let it cool, then peel off the paper backing.

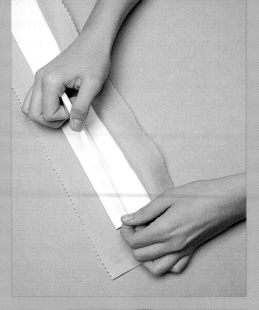

Now flip one side of the fabric over the poster board, covering the HeatnBond strip, and press with an iron for 4 to 6 seconds. Place a piece of HeatnBond over the fabric and follow the same steps. Fold over the other side of the fabric and iron down. Repeat these steps for the other tieback.

GLUE TEDDY BEARS

Turn your tieback over with the top facing you and fold it in half. Gather your teddy bears (we've used three here) and hot-glue them to the center of one-half of the fabric. Sew the plastic rings to each end of the tiebacks. Screw the cup hook into the window frame molding and you're ready to put them up.

teddy bear shelf liner

WHAT YOU'LL NEED

Brown craft paper or paper bags

Tape measure

Tracing paper

Pencil

Scissors

Hole punch

Measure the length and depth of your shelf. Add 3 to 4 inches to the depth of the paper for the decorative edge. Place the paper on your shelf and fold over and make a crease for the edge. With tracing paper, create a pattern for the scalloped edge using the pattern on this page.

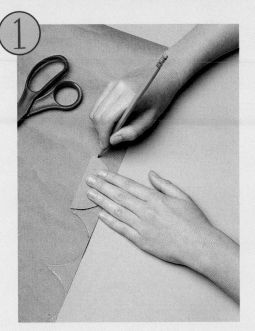

Trace the scallop onto the edge of your craft paper and cut out.

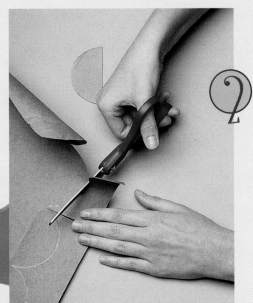

Snip! Snip!

Once all the scallops are cut, punch holes across the length of the paper.

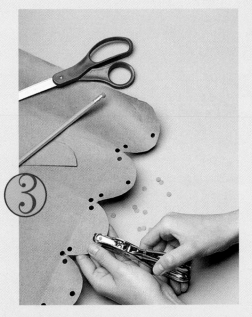

teddy bear picture hanger

WHAT YOU'LL NEED

3 to 5 small wooden photo frames (different sizes)

½" or ¾" round dowel rod, cut 16" to 18" long (ours is 18" long)

2 knobs for the ends of the dowel rod

Acrylic paint: light brown

Paintbrush

Scissors

5 yards of pink grosgrain ribbon

Hot glue gun and glue

E6000 adhesive

1 wooden knob with screw back (you can use a drawer pull)

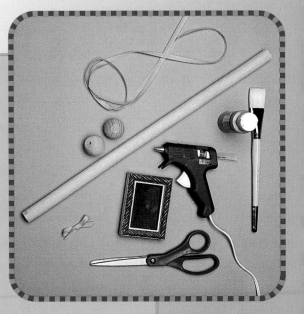

Let's Get Started

 Paint the photo frames, dowel rod, and dowel knobs with two coats of light brown paint. Let them dry between coats. Put your favorite photos inside the frames.

 Cut different lengths of ribbon to attach the frames to the dowel rod. (We cut them 12, 15, and 18 inches long.)

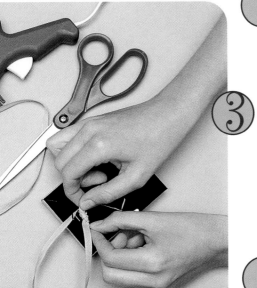

 Attach ribbon to the back of each frame with hot glue so ribbon will stay in place.

 Make small bows and hot-glue them to the front of the frames.

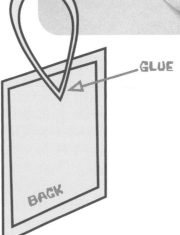

 Place the frames on the dowel rod and glue a knob to each end of the rod with E6000 adhesive. Let dry. Take the rest of the ribbon and tie to each end of the dowel rod for the hanger.

Pick a great spot on your wall and screw in the knob. Now arrange your frames from side to side to make the dowel hang level.

GLUE

BACK

teddy bear hammock

WHAT YOU'LL NEED

- 2 wooden dowels, ½" wide
- 4 wooden 1" dowel knobs
- Ruler or tape measure
- Acrylic paint: pink and white or cream
- Paintbrush
- 2 yards natural canvas
- Scissors
- HeatnBond iron-on glue tape or sewing machine with an adult's help!
- Iron
- Kitchen sponge
- Tracing paper
- Pencil or black marker
- Biodegradable foam plates
- Paper towels
- E6000 adhesive
- 2 yards of wide grosgrain ribbon
- 2 large cup hooks
- 2 medium S hooks
- Teddy bears of all shapes and sizes (we know you have lots of these!)

1. Cut the two dowel rods 12 inches long. Paint the dowel rods and knobs with two coats of white or cream paint, letting them dry between coats.

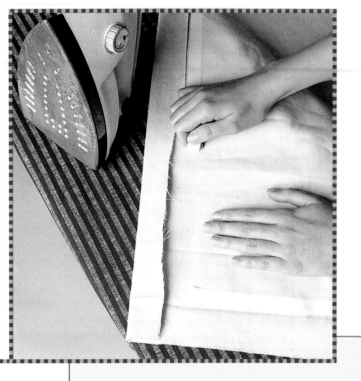

2. Cut the canvas 24 inches wide and 1 yard long. Make a 1-inch hem all the way around the canvas, using HeatnBond and an iron to secure it (see package for instructions). Fold each end over 3 to 4 inches and use HeatnBond to create a tunnel for the dowel rods. If you prefer, you can use a sewing machine instead of HeatnBond.

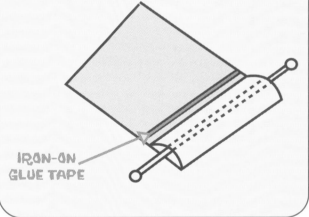

IRON-ON GLUE TAPE

3. Use tracing paper to make a heart-shape pattern from the design found at left and trace on the sponge with a pencil or black marker. Cut out the heart shape from the sponge.

4 Soak the sponge with water and squeeze until slightly damp. Pour the pink paint onto the foam plate; then dip the sponge into the paint and blot onto a paper towel. Turn the canvas over with the hem facing up. Press the heart onto the canvas hem and repeat along the lengths of the canvas, top and bottom. Let dry overnight.

5 Slip the dowels into the fabric and scrunch evenly. Attach the dowel knobs with E6000 adhesive. Let dry overnight. Attach pink ribbon to each end and hang the hammock to the wall using cup hooks and S hooks. Grab your favorite teddy bears and put them into their new home.

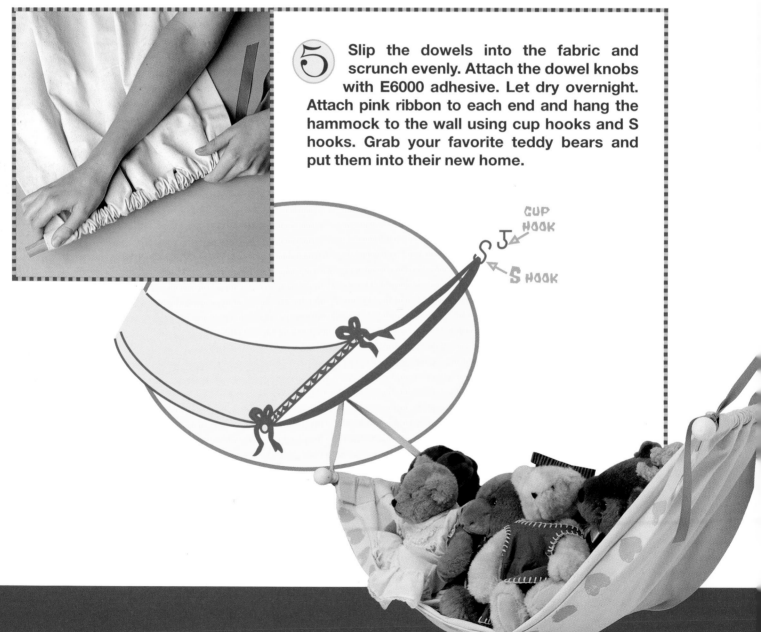

CUP HOOK

S HOOK

TEDDY BEAR Wastebasket

WHAT YOU'LL NEED

Old trash can or discarded popcorn tin or ice-cream tub

White spray paint

Bear-themed wrapping paper, cards, stationery, etc.

Scissors

Decoupage medium, such as Mod-Podge

Wide foam brush

Pink grosgrain ribbon, 1" to 1½" wide, long enough to go around the top of the trash can

Craft glue

Let's Get Started

1 Spray-paint the tin with two coats of white paint, letting it dry between coats. After the second coat, let it dry completely, preferably overnight.

2 Cut out your favorite teddy bear photos from cards, magazines, or wrapping paper. Use the decoupage medium, such as Mod-Podge, to glue the photos over the entire tin, overlapping them. Let dry overnight.

3 Brush a coat of decoupage medium over the entire tin of bears. Don't worry: It looks awful but will dry perfectly clear. Let it dry overnight.

4 Measure and cut the pink ribbon so it fits around the top of the tin. Glue it into place with craft glue.

You're definitely

a hip chick. Pure MTV, black, silver, gel, and tattoos, that's you. If you wear it, make it part of your room with our "Funky Chick" decor! Go crazy with hypercolors.

Funky Headboard

WHAT YOU'LL NEED

- Masonite or Fome-Cor board
- Ruler or tape measure
- Sandpaper
- Black paint

- Marvy metallic paint markers: silver, copper, gold, lime green, pink, turquoise
- Color photocopies of favorite pop stars or photos of friends

- Peel 'n Stick double-sided adhesive sheets (crafts store)
- Scissors
- Picture-frame hooks and small nails
- Hammer

Let's Get Started

 1 Prepare your headboard following the step #1 directions for the headboard on page 5.

2 Paint your board black. Don't forget those edges! Paint two coats, letting it dry between coats. Let it dry completely, preferably overnight. Here's a tip: If you use Fome-Cor board, paint both sides—it keeps it from warping.

3 To create this funky border, grab several metallic markers and draw different shapes and squiggle designs around the edges. Make color copies of words from magazines. You can even blow them up on a copier.

4 Put Peel 'n Stick on the back of the photos and words and cut them out with scissors. Peel off the backing and stick the photos and words to your headboard. Note: Glue can be used to mount the photos, but we found that it makes them wrinkle, and the black shows through. Using Peel 'n Stick looks a lot better.

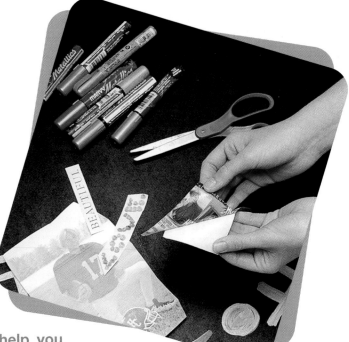

5 Get your mom or dad to help you attach your headboard to the wall.

Cool Spattered Wall

WHAT YOU'LL NEED

Latex wall paint: purple, magenta, orange, lime green, and turquoise

Large (6" wide) outdoor paintbrush

Drop cloths and newspapers

Masking or paint tape

Let's Get Started

Invite several friends over and have a paint party. Just dip your big floppy brush into colors of latex paint and fling! Cover everything you don't want spattered—like windows, doors, closets, furniture, and you!—with newspapers and drop cloths. Tape the newspapers and drop cloths where necessary.

NOTE TO PARENTS: Latex paint spatters will leave a texture on the wall when dry. After your daughter grows out of this look, you'll want to wallpaper.

Glam Treasure Box

WHAT YOU'LL NEED

Cardboard pencil or cigar box

Black acrylic paint

1" foam brush

Plastic jewels in various sizes

Jewel glue

Let's Get Started

Paint two or three coats of black paint on your cardboard box. Don't forget to paint the inside, too! Let it dry completely. Put a few drops of glue on the back of the jewels and cover the entire top. Be creative!!

Jewel glue is different from regular glue because it won't go cloudy on the back and dim your jewels' sparkle.

knobby jewelry hanger

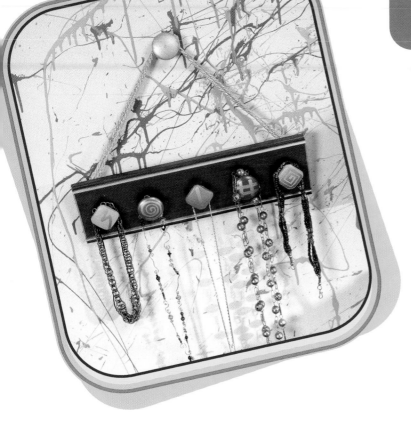

1 Paint the board and knobs with different metallic colors. Apply two or three coats of paint, allowing each coat to dry completely. Measure and space the knobs evenly across the board. Draw squiggly shapes on the knobs with the metallic paint markers. Glue into place with E6000 adhesive. Let dry for 24 hours.

2 Measure the rope to the length you want your board to hang. Hot-glue the rope to the back of the board. If you are hanging heavy pieces of jewelry, you may want to use small nails to hold the rope securely to the board.

3 Screw the wooden knob into the wall and you're ready to hang and add your jewelry.

WHAT YOU'LL NEED

Wood baseboard molding 18" to 20" long by 4" to 6" wide (or you can buy an unfinished plaque at a crafts store)

4 to 6 wooden cabinet knobs (round and square)

Ruler

Metallic acrylic paint or Marvy metallic paint markers: silver, copper, gold, lime green, pink, turquoise

Paintbrushes (small and medium sizes)

E6000 adhesive

Silver metallic rope trim

Hot glue gun and glue

Small nails

Hammer

1 wooden knob with screw back

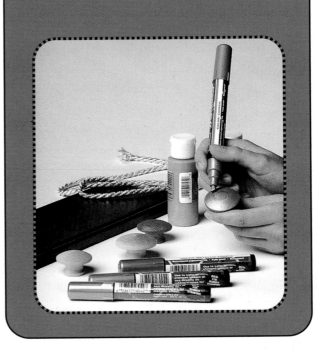

funky junky Window Topper

WHAT YOU'LL NEED

- Plywood valance or foam valance from fabric store
- Tape measure
- Medium-size nails
- Hammer
- Sandpaper
- Acrylic paint: metallic purple (or your favorite shocking color)
- Paintbrush
- Beads, old jewelry (great finds at garage sales and flea markets, or in an old junk drawer)— whatever you want to put on your valance
- Hot glue gun and glue
- E6000 adhesive

HEY YO!
Fun YO-YO Inc.

Way COOL!

3 Once the pieces are cut, nail them together. Use a fine grade of sandpaper to sand the edges and wipe with a soft cloth or old T-shirt. You don't have to be really fussy about how they go together since your topper will be covered with stuff anyway.

4 Paint your window topper with two coats of bright metallic purple (or use your favorite color). Let it dry between coats. Then, let it dry completely, preferably overnight.

5 Spread out all of your treasures, beads, feathers, old jewelry, whatever!

6 With the hot glue gun, attach all of your stuff in "layers" to cover the window topper! Looks like a party, doesn't it! Here's a tip: For heavier objects, use E6000 adhesive (read package instructions, because you'll need to let it dry for about 24 hours).

7 Get your mom or dad to help you hang up your valance with valance bracket hardware.

Let's Get Started

1 Purchase a foam window valance from a fabric store or home improvement store, or you can make your own from a piece of plywood.

2 If you use plywood, start by measuring the dimensions of your window. The length should be measured from the outside of the window molding on each side. The height of the valance can be from 10 to 12 inches, and it should stick out from the wall about 10 inches. Take these measurements to your local home improvement store or ask Mom or Dad to help you measure and cut out the pieces.

Funky Metallic Chair

WHAT YOU'LL NEED

Wood chair

Newspapers or a drop cloth

Spray can of silver metallic chrome paint

Metallic acrylic paint or Marvy metallic paint markers: pink, purple, yellow, lime green, orange, turquoise

Paintbrushes

Low-tack masking tape (from craft or home improvement store)

Spray away

Let's Get Started

1 Use soap and warm water to clean the chair. Let it dry completely. Put the chair in a well-ventilated area, either outdoors or in the garage. Place newspapers or a drop cloth under it. Shake the spray can well and spray the entire chair with two coats of paint, letting it dry between coats. Then, let it dry completely, preferably overnight.

2 Using the photo to the right as a guide, paint the spindles, back, and legs of the chair with metallic paint or paint markers.

3 If you use acrylic paint instead of the markers, you'll want to use low-tack masking tape to tape off the areas you want to remain silver. "Low tack" means it's not too sticky, so it won't pull off the silver paint you've already sprayed on the chair. Apply two coats of paint, letting it dry between coats. Let it dry completely before removing the masking tape.

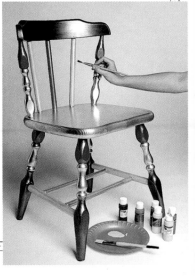

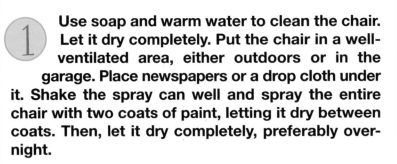

FuNKy BuLLetiN BoaRd

Cork bulletin board

Silver metallic spray paint

3 yards of ⅜" silver metallic ribbon

Silver upholstery tacks

Black paint marker

Newspapers

Hammer

Picture-frame hooks and nails

Let's Get Started

① You'll want to work in a well ventilated area, either outdoors or in the garage. Place newspapers under the bulletin board. Shake the spray can well and spray the entire bulletin board with two coats of paint, letting it dry between coats. Then let it dry completely, preferably overnight.

② Add a decorative edge with the black paint marker.

③ Attach the ribbon to the board with the silver upholstery tacks in a diamond design over the fabric. Trim the ribbon as you go. Use the diagram at left as a guide for tacking the ribbon onto the board.

Memories of camp, woodland projects, and adventures in the great outdoors are all around you. Thinking about becoming a vet or a forest ranger? Our "Nature Girl" room is like living in a jungle or the rain forest you'd like to save, with critters all around.

Girl

Masonite or Fome-Cor board

Ruler or tape measure

Sandpaper

Tissue paper in different shades of green

Pencil

Scissors

Decoupage medium, such as Mod-Podge

Biodegradable foam plate

Paintbrush

Leaves from yard: maple, oak, etc.

Hot glue gun and glue

Small nails and picture-frame hooks

Hammer

nature
HEADBOARD

Let's Get Started

① Grab your friends and take a hike—a nature hike!! Gather lots of leaves in different shapes and sizes.

② Prepare your headboard following the step #1 directions for the headboard on page 5.

③ To make tissue leaves, trace the real leaves onto green tissue paper. Cut them out.

4 Pour decoupage medium onto a foam plate and brush it onto your headboard—just do a small area at a time. Add the tissue paper leaves to the headboard. Make sure to overlap them so all of the board is covered. Keep adding leaves until the headboard is completely covered. Let dry.

5 Hot-glue a few real leaves on top of the tissue paper leaves.

6 Have Mom or Dad help you attach your headboard to the wall using nails and picture-frame hooks.

nature bookends

WHAT YOU'LL NEED

Large rocks

Large paint markers in bright colors

Let's Get Started

1 Wash your rocks with dish detergent and put them out in the sun to dry.

2 Use several brightly colored paint markers to decorate the rocks with bugs or sayings like: Save the Earth, Flowers Are Fun, Bugs Are Beautiful, I ♥ Nature. Or make up your own!!!

3 You can also use these great rocks as doorstops or paperweights.

FERN PRINT Window Shade

cool

WHAT YOU'LL NEED

Variety of leaves from outdoors: fern, maple, oak, etc.

White vinyl shade

Acrylic paints: 4 shades of green

Biodegradable foam plates

Paintbrushes

Paper towels

Let's Get Started

① Go hiking with friends and gather up lots of leaves like fern, maple, oak, etc. Spread out your shade and weight it down with books so the edges don't roll up (flap, flap, flap . . . !).

② Pour several shades of green paint onto foam plates and paint the back side of each leaf, making sure you have plenty of paint on the leaves. ────────────

③ Press the leaf onto the shade, paint side down. ────────────

④ Place a folded paper towel over the top of the leaf. Press down with even pressure over the leaf, making sure that all of the leaf is printed onto the shade. Repeat these steps, using different leaves and different shades of green paint until your shade is completely covered. Let the shade dry 24 hours before rolling it up. ────────────

⑤ Get your mom or dad to help you hang up your shade.

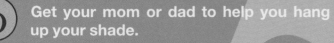

WHAT YOU'LL NEED

Variety of leaves from outdoors: fern, maple, oak, etc.

Vinyl flooring piece cut to desired size

Newspapers or a drop cloth

Acrylic paints: cream and 4 shades of green

Polyurethane sealer

OPTIONAL:

Acrylic paints: red, pink, and yellow

2" foam brushes

Biodegradable foam plates

Paper towels

Kitchen sponges

Colored markers

nature floorcloth

Let's Get Started

1. First, collect a variety of leaves. Then put newspapers or a drop cloth under your piece of vinyl to protect the floor around you. Note: Put the flooring on the drop cloth front side down. You'll be working on the back side of the vinyl flooring and not the front! (Weird, huh?) Paint the entire surface with cream acrylic paint. Let it dry completely and brush on a second coat. Let it dry overnight.

2. Pour different shades of green paint onto foam plates. Paint the back side of the leaves. This is where you can really see the veins and details of the leaf. You'll want to make sure you have plenty of paint on the leaves.

3. Place the leaf on the floor mat with the painted side of the leaf down.

4. Place a folded paper towel over the top of the leaf. Press down with even pressure over the leaf, making sure that all of the leaf is printed onto the floor mat. Repeat these steps, using different leaves and different shades of green paint until your floor mat is completely covered. Let it dry completely, preferably overnight.

5. Use a wide black paint marker to create a wavy border around the edges of the mat.

6. Let it dry at least 24 hours and then spray on two coats of a polyurethane sealer. Let it dry completely between each coat.

OPTIONAL

We decorated our floor mat with bugs, snails, and butterflies created by cutting kitchen sponges into lopsided hearts and circles—hearts for the butterflies, and circles for the ladybugs and snails. Soak the sponges in water and squeeze until slightly damp. Pour paint—yellow and pink for the butterflies and snails, and red for the ladybugs—onto a foam plate and press the sponge into the paint and then on your floor mat. Let them dry completely. Add the critter details with black and colored paint markers.

Butterfly bulletin board

WHAT YOU'LL NEED

Bulletin board

Green moss (from crafts store)

Hot glue gun and glue

Silk butterflies, ferns, and leaves

Raffia: cream, green, or natural

Quick-dry clay or polymer clay

Knife

Paint markers: black and red

Thumbtacks

E6000 adhesive

bugs!

MOSS

RIBBONS...

1. Hot-glue green moss around the frame of the bulletin board. Add butterflies, ferns, and leaves to the moss with the hot glue gun. Tie a raffia bow around a few fern leaves or branches and glue to the corner of your board.

butterflies

beetles

BOWS!

PLANTS?

2. To create the ladybug pushpins, roll the clay into balls about the size of the head of a thumbtack and flatten with your finger to create the bug. Cut a Y design on the back with a knife. Let dry. Paint the body with a red paint marker and use the black marker to add the head and dots. Use E6000 adhesive to glue the ladybug to the thumbtack. Hang your bulletin board on the wall and add all your important stuff.

Memory Tree

WHAT YOU'LL NEED

Dried tree branch that's shaped like a tree (4 to 5 feet tall)

Large clay pot

Plaster of Paris (mixed according to package instructions)

Mementos to hang on tree: leaves, pinecones, birdhouses, bird's nests, wind chimes, etc.

Grosgrain ribbon, ¼" wide, or embroidery yarn

Scissors

Green moss

Let's Get Started

1 Find a large tree branch that's shaped like a small tree.

2 You'll want your best friend to help you with this project. Put the tree branch into a large clay pot. While she holds the tree in the pot, pour the plaster of Paris mixture around the tree branch, filling the pot about three-fourths of the way. Then prop the tree straight, because the plaster will need to set overnight.

3 Gather up all your treasured mementos, or create some that go with the nature theme. You can decorate the tree branch with leaves, pinecones, birdhouses, bird's nests, angels, and wind chimes made of twigs and seashells . . . just let your imagination go crazy. Hang them on the tree with ribbon or embroidery yarn.

4 To finish off your tree, put green moss around its base.

Teddy Bears

this is the template for the vine

this is the template for the paw print

this is the template for the flower

NOTE: Trace at 100% or adjust sizes using a photocopier

EMPLATES • T

FloWer PoWer

this is the template for the flower petals

① 1

this is the template for the flower insides

② 2

NOTE:
Trace at 100%
OR
adjust sizes
using a photocopier